Sometimes all you need to do is...

TAKE A DEEP BREATH

By: Kristen Schmitt

Little Blue Ink

Take a Deep Breath Copyright @2020 Kristen Schmitt
ISBN: 979-8-587808485

Take a Deep Breath is written by Kristen Schmitt and Illustrated by Aldila Permata
All rights reserved. No part of this book may be reproduced in any form without permission in writing from the author.

Published by:
Little Blue Ink
www.littleblueink.com

Take another deep breath when you catch the flu

Take a deep breath if you start to cry

You see, sometimes things don't go our way—
but the good news is... that's okay!

If your day doesn't go quite as planned

Be happy to know that you can start all over again

Your best will change from day to day

Even those who might be your foe

Just remember you are loved in special ways

So, take a deep breath to relax your mind

Take a deep breath because it enhances your mood

Just to be reminded of how you are great.
Great, Great, Great!

THE END

Made in the USA
Las Vegas, NV
13 October 2023